AF571723

THE RED FOX

THE RED FOX

Happiness is egg-shaped.
And I know all about chickens.

BILL HOWELL

McCLELLAND and STEWART LIMITED
Toronto / Montreal

ACKNOWLEDGEMENTS

Many thanks to the following
people who gave me encouragement,
publication, and money when
I needed it:

Alphabet
another poetry magazine
The Book Cellar Anthology
The Canada Council
Canadian Broadcasting Corporation
Canadian Forum
Dalhousie Review
either/or
Fiddlehead
Made In Canada
Performing Arts In Canada
Prism international
Quarry
Soundings
Storm Warning
Tamarack Review
Vigilante

0-7710-4241-8

THE CANADIAN PUBLISHERS
McClelland and Stewart Limited
25 Hollinger Road, Toronto 374

Beverley

CONTENTS

ANTHEM

And men all over the earth
  asked their women to dance
    with them.

And with song it was said,
  for there is nothing closer
    to your soul than your breath.

THE MAGICIAN'S WIFE

This month she's on the road with him,
so in the trailer backstage she's got coffee
brewing, but now she only gives us glimpses
of her excellence, and leaves us wondering
whether or not she helps him to escape.

What do they talk about between sets?

We, the audience, invent each trick,
and each trick invents its own ritual,
but she's the one who appears to pause
between our every breath, for hers
is a living made on sleights, a trick
performed just less than once too often.

How old will they grow together?

No one believes in his illusion more
than the woman he loves, for she knows
it's not at all what he does, but how, from
a new trick performed first for her only
to an old one, great with its necessity
for perfect public execution.

But does she know his secret to everything?

Just offstage, she stares at him, masculine
as magic, until he leaves with our applause
and the awful promise of what he hasn't shown
us, this one
true friend of cards and silks
and doves.

HORSEWOMAN

Fine lady, choosing
horse and husband,
where your wish goes
I go with you. . . .

Often, even now you
wave your white
hand at my
horizon. . . .

Then you
go, the grey day our distance, our
spring,
the season between

Good Friday and good
weather, the seawind

winding in your hair, with
the smell of animal upon,

below your leather
clothes, with

the fluid hugeness
clamped between
your thighs. . . .

INTERPRETING A SMILE

Lust is held in manmade place
by trust. Trust me to write
a poem about you/another man's
wife. But I've been watching you move
from my distance. . . .

You grin across your office at me, your
bare breasts moving
under your sweater over there. Are your ends
irritated by some fabrics? Do you
know what I mean?

(Yes, even we have a conspiracy.)

Watching you move is like winding up
my wristwatch without thinking about it.
I can almost taste the fingerprints
on your salads. Your body is as firm
as the core of any planet. Today I will live
forever/tie myself to your sun
and the sea inside me. . . .

Tonight I will imagine you with me.
There will be a man with a public
expression on his face sitting at the table
across the room from us. I will stare
at your strong shoulders when you
are down there with me in your mouth.
And when the man and the public expression
have gone, the world will end with your legs
wrapped around my neck. . . .

And still you move, trying to ignore me
not ignoring you. . . .

And oh, that sweet, sweet smile!

JANE'S WHY-GLASSES

We're eating toasted
bacon-lettuce-tomato
sandwiches
alone together
in the S.U.B. cafeteria
at our special now-table
and I
say something about anything
and she
blinks beautifully and grabs
for her why-glasses.

SHYNESS

I'm still bothering myself about the slush
I've just shaken off the cuffs of my corduroys
and out of my shoes
                                        when I enter the bedroom
blowing my December cold hands. . . .

The blankets trace your shape, the shape of you
and your edgeless dream. . . .

MECHANICS OF LIVING

Becoming each other with flattering and swearing
words with yellow endings, you lie
towards me with decency
enough to make love, while I
leave my glasses on to see you better
from my distance, running the risk
of breaking them
while we bury ourselves
in this process.

BEFORE A MIRROR

This is the old woman
who owns the mirror:
she defines her love
by her distance from it.

Its frame surrounds her
like wet wood smoke.

At its centre her face,
like anyone's, is public
domain, but her image
is reflected in her eyes,
reflected again in mine.

We are both so sure,
no matter what we do,
the mirror will not shatter.

Twice the distance from never,
she has never been as far
away from anyone before:
her frame surrounds my age
like wet wood smoke.

EYE SONG

How does she
see me? The plans
I make in bed
are all there
in her eyes. This
is when she
fears me most
because I'm wrong
so often. But always
it seems I may be
right this time,
so she waits to see
if I'll fall back
alive in her arms
again alive in my
unsuccess. How can I
ever hold her here
with my eyes?

RE-ELECTION POEM

(How I Eventually Get To Sleep At Night
By Becoming Something Of A Politician)

Every night I have to win an extended debate
of arms, elbows, shoulders, toenails, knees, and
legs, our lips too tired to keep on talking.

The outcome is sometimes often in doubt,
like when she wants to try to get to sleep
by lying like spoons in a drawer together.

But we always ultimately end up facing facts
and each other's backs, since that's the only
way that ever seems to work.

So we burrow into sleep, each on our own right
side of the dark in the bed, but then, over there,
there's always a moaning whimper demanding concessions.

I'm usually feeling generous enough to bend
my left knee back behind me to kiss
her calf with the sole of my foot.

Then she's nearly content to maintain contact
with her right hand resting warm and dry here
on my hip for what she believes may be forever.

And even when I'm dreaming, I'm half-aware of her
turning herself back around, electing me again
in her sleep with her hands in my hair.

I MISSED YOU

Mostly, it was the morning
the orange juice ran out
and the two-week bed needed
changing. Not that you
were such a good housekeeper:
I always tidied up things.
But there were a few things
I'd gotten out of the habit of
doing. I could wait 'til eight-
thirty, when the I.G.A. opened,
and buy a few things
like orange juice, but I don't
think I'll remember forgetting
that with one person in it,
a bed doesn't stay cleaner
twice as long.

MY WORLD

Is in the back seat with
the Heat turned on HIGH while
the snow quietly collects itself
on the roof and windows before
we have to go home.

                                There's a war
on the radio, but it's dead
for now. . . .

Some of us are lovers.
And some are warriors.

                                  Either way –
I am not a warrior.
I die all the time.

                            There are no objections. . . .

FIRST POEM FOR ANOTHER WOMAN

I am the man your last lover warned you about.

Our love will become the warmed-over memory of last night's
curry dinner, because I'll tell you inevitable lies.

I will even buy you lunch again at the *Hind Quarter*
so you can stare back at me and notice my impeccable
table manners, but I'll never tip the waitress.

I will marvel you with more inventive stories, packed
with convincing details, to make myself more of an enigma
to you.

            I will get out of bed in the middle of the night
and write poems about you to persuade both of us
that you are the loveliest woman in the world.

                                                            You will be
convinced that I'm the noblest, honestest
man in the world, even if you know I'm only that way
with you.

            I will tell you I love you because I don't
know where what comes out of me comes from.

                                                            I will push
to lose myself in you, but I'll be painfully gentle,
because I'll be more afraid of what we might find out
than you.

            I will probably try to see God in your eyes
when I'm propped up on my elbows and moving slowly in
and out of you.

            I will close my eyes and make your
shoulder raw with my beard when I bury my head there,
and my sweat will smell like a man's sweat to you.

You will drown the bed with your love for me, and I
will spit myself into your pillow.

I will try not to
dream or hope too much for you, and I will tell you that I love you
because I do, and your last lover will be right.

AFTER WORDS

She's over there
apart for now
so you can come
together better
later. . . .

By now you've learned words
are not enough.

You mix music with friends
instead of phrases.

And you've loved enough to sing
about it afterwards.

DROWNING MAN

Life flashes past
my mind's eyes. . . .

I know what I
haven't done.

Why do you ask
if I love you?

FROM THIS HEADLAND

Merigomish Harbour, Pictou Co., N.S.

Now's the time for the air to roll
in sweet and sweaty with the gravity
of fog and tide from beyond
the collapsing sky.

The coast, the memory of the life
that was, begins its slide
slowly under the time that lives
below each day's horizon.

The sail is trimmed and scratched again
for another older unforgotten wind
because the sea insists that we remember.
Every tide is always new, always

overdue, and time cracks hard and sharp
above our deck as they come-about again
to test their right to ride the crest
of another wave of night.

Once a night, as in the day, the sea
feeds on this land, the land where even now
no map or chart is ever accurate or sure for more
time than it takes to watch the next new tide.

And now the dusk's complete, the land
leans into the night and turns in-
to the sea which breathes its life
away, and the wind expires.

There's always what applies out there
apart from what applies on shore,
and now, without a wind, without a sky,
the world is dead and wandering.

All men about tonight are apparitions,
each owned alone by too many tides, men
who've died to plow the waves for answers,
who no longer know what must be known.

I imagine them still out there,
never home until they've landed,
their knots of eyesight now untied
from the safety of their tiny mooring lamps.

And their voices, saddened by distance,
groan and overcome the quiet question
of the full night tide, and challenge the fog
with new warnings and old memories.

TWO NORTH SHORE TIDES

1.

Daily I fish
away
hour tide waters
for
last minute minnows
with
second chance hooks.

2.

Try overlooking the ocean.

And wonder why a wave
is bigger than a beach

yet a beach can take
so many waves.

A YEAR AGO TODAY

(For Johnny MacPherson, Dr. Bill Bittner,
Herb Lewis, Tessie Gillis, Tor Haines,
Jean-Claude, Ernie, Eve, the Town of Wolf-
ville, Janie, Lynx, Rubin Broome, Brother
Bob, Trevor the dog, and anyone else who
sometimes puts in tenders to salvage
things.)

Country Joe Carver, black as night,
and John-Angus, who can't swim, and Willie R. Fraser, his father,
who only deals in war surplus or stolen goods, put in
a tender to salvage the *Carson Chalmers* after she sank
with a full load of something-or-other off Hantsport.

(I remember it exactly, 'cause it was the same week
I took the dog over to Marty MacPherson's in Curry's Corner
in my Ford to breed to his bitch for twenty bucks and a case
of Moosehead beer, the idea being that Marty would sell
the puppies, but that's another story.)

Now, Willie R. only prays when he wants something
so bad he can't think of anything else to do, and then
an idea hits him, 'specially when he's been off the booze
so long it seems like forever he's been on vanilla extract.

Must've been something like that when he saw the ad
in the Chronicle-Herald and started asking 'round, and found out
all the regular salvage companies had checked out the operation
with those preliminary explorations of theirs, and figured
the *Carson Chalmers* was a lost cause, see.

Only, Country Joe had his surplus store.
He makes a business out of hanging onto things
people never even know they'll ever need, and no one
can figure out how a man who sings as much as Country Joe
can be so mean: soon as anyone even mentions his name
you just gotta know you're in for something diabolical.

And John-Angus, he's just bad, spends all his time bragging
'bout the time he and the Sampson boys from Hall's Harbour
got drinking and beat up on the whole town of Port Williams
at the Fire Hall one Saturday night, then got away
before the Mounties got there. Wouldn't be so bad
if it wasn't so true.

People say Willie R. must have something
on Country Joe, otherwise they wouldn't hang 'round so much
together. God knows they're both such good friends
they'd both cheat themselves sooner than each other, they say,
but you've gotta have a look at them grinning to know
they've done enough to themselves. At any rate,
nobody beats Willie R. at getting good deals and prices
at Country Joe's up there in Lower Falmouth.

So they said it just couldn't be done, not even
with thirty thousand dollars, a crew of sixty,
and a bad month. Not ever, but they didn't figure
on Country Joe's store, John-Angus' mouth, or Willie R.'s prayers.
"Three thousand dollars," wrote Willie R.,
with his notorious hand, "and three days." As usual,
no one knew too much about it. I mean, everyone knew
they were going to do it, but no one knew exactly how,
since there was no mention of men, and you have to be crazy
to get in with that bunch.

I can only suppose Willie R. couldn't quite have been too particular
and was probably just glad to have anybody when
John-Angus called in the Sampson boys.

(Now I know from the time I was over there that
the Sampson place isn't really comfortable 'less half the boys
are in jail, 'cause there's eight of them and only
the four beds – if there's more than the four there's always trouble –
but there were six of them home there then, "between jobs,"
so maybe that's where your answer is.)

Now John-Angus, being Willie R.'s boy, could take care
of himself, but he always had the Sampson boys with him
when he was ever onto something important, and he plainly
thought the job was important, or so he told everyone,
but that was all. "It's an important job"
was all he'd say. I heard him say it that first day
they got the job and the advance for "General Expenses"
from Porter's, when he was on his way to the Liquor
Commission to fetch some rum for his father.

Worst thing you can ever do is laugh at a man
who needs a drink, 'cause that's what makes him
go out and get it. Even John-Angus had his shoes off
feeding lines to the Sampson boys, who were busy
fixing things up. Willie R. sat right there on a folding chair
with his rum bottle beside him, on that barge they rented
from Charlie McCann, yelling instructions from a bunch of notes
and drawings he had in one of those little black school scribblers.

Had to yell 'cause the Sampson boys were all in the water
there, and 'cause Country Joe was busy cussing and swearing
he was gonna get everybody if it didn't work, even if Willie R.
was his best friend and customer, 'cause they were putting on wear
to his fifty-odd good, surplus Navy rubber dinghies, just
getting them wet. It just damn well wouldn't work, he screamed,
and everyone watching out onto the Basin from the wharf there
agreed with him for the first time in their lives.

Now the dinghies the Sampson boys were using were all tied
together, empty of air, 'round the *Carson Chalmers*, with the triggers
on the pressured air containers all fixed together on one
pull-string affair, see, set to go off all at once
when Willie R. said. It took them two days to fix things
right, then Willie R. said they had to wait for high tide.

Word got 'round that morning that something was up,
and since everybody's interested when somebody's doing something,
we were all there watching. Everybody from West Gore to Port Lor
even the Creighton boys from Gaspereaux, who probably got cheated
worse than any with those two jeeps, was all there to see the day
when Willie R. Fraser was gonna go down.

About noon, while the Sampson boys stood 'round
with their hands on their hips, Willie R. took a long
series of gulps from his bottle, said a quick but significant
prayer, and pulled the rope to the air below him.

Nothing at all happened for a good minute, but then,
slow and shaky, the *Carson Chalmers* rose from the dead
and Country Joe stopped swearing.

A couple of days after, Porter's paid off, and that's when
the real trouble started. After General Expenses, there was
fifteen hundred and twenty dollars clear. Everyone heard that.
It seemed that Country Joe and Willie R. both agreed that
John-Angus should pay the Sampson boys from his share, since
they were his friends. But John-Angus figured the Sampson boys
ought to be deducted from General Expenses, and to prove
his point, he looked 'round, grabbed a handy wooden pop crate
and threw it at his father's head.

He was a smart boy: as usual, the Sampson boys all
ended up in jail for the winter, and even with their lumps,
the three of them – County Joe, John-Angus, and Willie R. –
have been drinking up the money ever since.

And that's the way things stand, except
that was year ago exactly, see, so the Sampson boys
get out this week, and nobody can wait to see.

THE HANDLE OF TOMORROW

Will I lie
quietly with an arrow
in my heart, my body growing cold
without my words, however true,
to warm me?

CENTRELEA, ANNAPOLIS COUNTY:
And still today I come after Blood Creek
with the record of the water running
thick and scarlet in the sun –
a day away from Acadia.
The report of the day is in my hands,
and its arrows, pounding in the air,
sort themselves out – this for another,
this one for me.

This was the French side
        with the Micmacs with their dogs.
That was this English side
        with the water running quicker with the ambushed drums
toward the greater sea of meetings
as it does as I stand alone
        with other arrows flying here.

I become my own history watching itself:
the well-appointed Red of my forefathers marching
in strict time toward my time, now
back with the blood Red Micmacs moving
stealthily – at least, I know now, the Micmacs
of the mind.

All of us surely die in our own way,
a matter of our own matter, this time:
June 10, 1711. My arrow.
Quicker, stronger, straighter the always shaft,
always unseen comings
and goings.

Then the question of the captive and the wounded . . .
WHAT ALWAYS HAPPENS?
. . . the torture of the mind in killing, dying in ideas
of ourselves and freedoms from forevers and infinities
of pain – the joy acclaims itself, if we live.

CAPE BLOMIDON, KING'S COUNTY:
And still today I come before Glooscap
where I look down at where I study
the Micmac god and warrior chieftain. HE
is fiercer than fierce, blood redder than any
brothers, mightier and truer, higher
and low, and dead.

Can I, perhaps, escape
stealthily,
into the fur forests of fortune?
Or run beside their memory
like an Indian dog
with a bloody Red Coat soldier's right
arm clamped firmly
in my jaws?

ONE-ARMED MAN

Met him at the Ferry Wharf,
from his sinister eyes I saw
he'd been to sea and left
at least behind his only right
arm: home for good now, from the Banks now
punching tickets for Dominion Atlantic
in his left behind hand way.

Before the everybody question came
from my gut to my mouth I heard
the answer in his face: nothing's in a name,
but his face, a fifty-bucks-a-week the hard way face,
while his eyes sang with the bitter salt of the sea,
breaking on its ocean motion moving rock,
breaking on its own image.

Every time I'm by I buy
my ticket from this man,
give him a second hand, and
face the feeling I've been
cheated.

AT THE HORSESHOE TAVERN

The woman on the Mountain
is eighteen, and she
comes down to shop
at the Wolfville Save-Easy
every Friday night (where you
can meet her if you want), and she
has two kids under three
a husband in Dorchester Penitentiary
smokes Rothman's cigarettes
owns a turquoise pantsuit
remembers her cousins
collects Buck Owens records
makes the best rabbit stew
you ever tasted, and wants
to go to Toronto someday.
You should see her then.

OLD CHARLIE

Old Charlie would walk beside himself
    along the Wolfville dyke, way out
by the part where the cow died last
    August, catching his rum bottle
in his armpit, inside his rusty tweed
    coat, and pause for a nip every now
and then, pretending no one knew
    he was there, proudly unsober, and open
to the stink of missing memories.

MORNING SMOKE

Sitting on differences,
smoke and blue sky day clouds, almost
lost in white, feet too
lazy for walking.

Handing out hellos, like
apples to good children, to friendly
neighbourly folks, munching by on shared smiles,
almost like friendly neighbours.

Staring at the stupid smoke, curling
the same way if it's from a first
cigarette from a new pack, or a spare
almost second last one from the last.

Wondering what'll happen to the sky,
the smiles, if someone strolls along, asks
the day and you if you have another
smoke or apple.

SAILMAKER

Late tonight with canvas
and tight twine he reefs
and reams his ageless light.

Upstairs his sons sleep
close with their wives and
latest plans for leaving.

His time and tomorrow's tide
will slide them all away
on seas of wind where maybe
they'll believe the best
of his billowing dreams.

FROM HALIFAX

This was the place
my parents chose
to make their home,
and when I was there
it was my
reality.

(What's the difference
between someone
you've never met
and a place
you've never been?)

Where you hope to go
someday is never
here until you know
what you hope
you've left
behind.

I go home to visit,
and remember why

SEVENTEEN FORTY-NINE

Who cares who we've been? Those without roots
will never forgive those of us with them. . . .

Weren't we the first Free Enterprisers here,
the ones who first helped haul the bells up
into old St. Paul's? Merchants from Bristol,
Portsmouth, and Liverpool, who came back
to the Banks with Cabot, and stayed
where "the fish slowed the progress
of our ships." The guys who laughed
at Humphrey Gilbert's plumes at St. John's
harbour, who made *money* while Hudson and Frobisher
were busy busting their asses for us. The guys
who were pressed into the Royal Navy, who turned
back the Armada. The guys who finally had enough
of England when England gave Louisbourg back, but
who went on anyway, because we've never run
from a fight we couldn't win, to take Quebec,
the Great Rock, the Key to All. . . . Pity
the poor WASP, who has to sting himself first. . . .

For don't we all make up our own histories
as we go, those of us who are "doing well"?

My father, bred and buttered in Portsmouth,
took me and my brother across the Great Sea
to this New World at ten months of age
from Abercrombie Hospital in Liverpool, and
we giggled and bawled the whole way over.
If that isn't formative, what is? My mother,
a Loyalist from St. John, lost her grandmother's
brooch playing Madame La Tour in high school,
and still loves to holiday in New England,
searching for distant, lost, Yankee relations.
And we all have cousins who hid the Expulsion out
in the Gaspereaux Hills. And cousins who gave
diesel oil to Nazi u-boats outside Lunenburg
just before I was born. . . . Pity the poor WASP,
who has to sting himself last. . . .

But how long have we been sleeping here,
beside our secret memory, the sea?

Too soon we seem old inside our trusty dream. . . .
("Ah yes, bye, and we'd do it all again, by God!")
Most important of the things that don't work
in this city are the guns on Citadel Hill. . . .
("And ah, she's a fine side, that one!")
And the noonday gun is just a vain attempt
to kill the rest of the afternoon. . . .
("And there's always some pretty lively
steppers in the distance. . . .")
There's a Zumburger stand in Scotia Square,
and nobody knows what *that* means. . . .
("And you can always tell a man from his hands.")
And all the old electric Beltline trolley buses,
outdated with so many other dates around,
have been sold for a *fine* price to Toronto. . . .
("And inland, bye, the continent starts from *here*!")
And here, bellbottoms will always be fashionable. . . .

So shall we sell them Tidal Power
or tell them seabirds rule the world?

IN THE WATER

I find that
blood clots
                    don't belong
sticking to flesh.
I find that swimming naked
in the ocean
                    is the same
for everyone,
but everything depends
on where
I find it.

THE LONG AND THE SHORT

It's the start of a new snowball.
It's crunching around in leaves in the old
fashioned places kids always seem to find
and grow up from. It's when everything's dead
as soon as it hits the backstop. It's how long
it's been since wondering what it's like up there
at the other end of the kitestring, the end
that never stops. It's a year ago.

BOYS AND DOGS

Boys bark, too. Twice I was the Black Fox,
and Charlie Richardson was the only guy allowed
to be it three times because he broke his arm,

and Hatfield, and Brother Bob, and Syd Dumaresq,
and Cammy Robinson, and Wilsie and Steve and
Denny Perlin and everyone

was Red or Blue or White or Yellow or Green
or Purple and even Silver or Gold Fox.

It was understood that we each took our own turn.

Arriving on blue-and-white CCM bikes
in any of three speeds with no licenses,
leaving Miss Ferguson's fraction problems behind
the whole unreasonable wonder of the woods. . . .

Other times we made the dogs play dead, dug holes
in the clearing in the part of the woods

behind Billy McKinnon's house, just when his mother
always seemed to have some new brown bread, and played

marbles. We spent whole mornings shooting glass balls
in the sunlight, and the game ended only

when there were too many rules, only
when it became necessary to name it.

Chopping and peeling up and down alders and our
Saturday mornings with soon-to-be-lost jack-knives,
chomping through ten o'clock apples
in not-so-secret spruce forts. . . .

Maybe it was because there were no girls allowed.

Maybe it was the girls that were our ultimate
discovery, the one that made the question of the game
hardly worth playing, afterwards.

Maybe we only made so many great discoveries
because there were greater ones to be made.

Maybe we did grow up in those Saturday suns,
and afternoons only came when each of us
found a different name for ourself.

telegram

DEAR SON
GIVE IT UP STOP
COME HOME STOP
WITH LOVE STOP
DAD

THE RAINY DAY ROAD SONG
(Unfinished)

Trudging on dog-nipped heels
in six-day socks
up another rainy hill
past another white house
and another picture window
while another fat girl watches
water into my head.

Slinking on padded claws
quiet in her house
shy behind her window
pausing on her drier hill
while a future of sorts
starts and stops
a panorama of wet innocence.

I came in from the rain
I came out of the rain
I came with the rain
while the road waited

FIRST CLASS JOURNEY

Mid-March weekend, searching
for the truth of north, two mad
city boys slide seventeen miles
on snowshoes over leftover melting
drifts, feet always sinking eight,
ten inches down, four feet down
to the forest floor, a memory.

Mid-morning, deer tracks and branch
nibblings, day birds, false trail
where moose has torn hole in woods,
trees brittle as ice on them, but
we warm up as the rhythm of day
takes over, make good time
in the good air.

Mid-afternoon, after time told by
sun and compass, map in our minds,
drenched to the waist, stop to camp
on nearest hill, plenty of spruce
cover, dry wood, look into twilight,
hurry, numb hands as the freeze
comes on fast.

Midnight, hot tea and twigs, close
by fire built on boulder, reflector
for the certain human heat, wrapped
in skins of animals, no words while
rabbits scamper across crust, now
six inches, and beyond our light
the stars, the Great Bear sleeps. . . .

THE FATHER AS MAN TO THE CHILD

for Dad

You came across your oceans
of thought and met and married
as if you had always been a man.

A man of science and heart, how
many times have you helped me
make myself over and better?

As a boy I played to be the man
I imagined you were.
                                        Moby Dick
in the afternoon, and Huck Finn
stuck to the Tar Baby before
I went to sleep. And afterwards
we had Hornblower in common. . . .

                                                            Images of you
on your office phone at home while
dinner was getting cold, or
swearing at me for being late
in the car on the way to being Warden
of St. Paul's Church in front
of my college girlfriend, and
understanding why

I loved my identical twin brother
in a way I could never reach you. . . .
Now I make up what I don't know
from what I know best. I am
never sure what I would say,
except, since they're my birth-
right from you, I would write
good words.

We have disagreed
about Shakespeare. You have said
living through a war has made you
more human, while I feel living
without one can mean more. Yes, even I
would compete with you. . . .

I believe in the things you've said
you have faith in. Like not making it
because you're an honest man. But
I have grown up to be unreserved.

In your youth you grew up to play
different games. It was incredible
that you could be on my side. And yet
there was sweet beauty in a ball
that came all the way from you.

You spent more time teaching me
how to throw than you did learning
me how to catch. . . .
I still need you
for that honesty. As a man I play
to be the boy you never showed me.

AFTER FINALLY READING CAMUS THROUGH TO THE END

All you great old men, sick
and stomping around your hermitages
like greater wounded bears,
drinking quart after quart of the basic acids,
belching Life with a capital "if,"
and lurching through the last of it,
for the record, you're wrong.

As soon as you say, "I think," you're gone.

Ah, so when you get old
you get selfish, eh?
And after a lifetime habit of giving?
Don't give me that!

My old man told me something once,
and for that once I was listening.
It was when I was at the rejecting everything stage,
You know, God and Jesus and the Church,
and split level homes and second cars and TV sets,
and first cars and TV sets, and everything,
and he said this:
"If you can't figure out what's what,
the hell with it. What's more important
is what you're going to do. Just do
what you feel is right, and what
you feel is good."

So I went downstairs to the basement
and grabbed ahold of my shirt
and found myself.
And came back up again.
And it was a long way both ways,
but here I am.

For the record again, I'll tell you all how
I'm going to end:
I'm ninety-seven
in my Ferrari on a Alpine roadway (or equivalents)
when I miss a hairpin
turn with my sixth or seventh wife, age 18,
beside me (again, or equivalents),
when a ball of living fire
crowns my charisma.

But you won't be around to see it, will you?

And all the headlines'll scream:
"HOWELLS'S VIRILITY REDUCED!" or "INTERNATIONAL STUD DUST!"
And everybody'll shake their head sadly,
and smile and say I died
best. . . .
Once more, with feeling!

I CAN'T WAIT TO GET HOME FOR CHRISTMAS AND BE HUGGED BY MOM

And tell her all about Dorothy
or whoever it is at the moment,
and string up eight-to-a-set Noma
lights out front in the rain,
and drive the family Chevy down
to Don Schelew's for dry cleaning
(mostly mine), and maybe cut off
my beard to please everybody
(including myself, because after all
my face really *is* interesting enough
by itself, and Uncle Gordon and
Auntie Madge will be able to recognize
me again), and for once not have to
borrow money from Dad or Brother Bob
to buy presents, and get a little
drunk and watch the NFL Pro Bowl Game
on the rec room TV, and just sit around
with a stupid grin, needing to be needed.

A LULLABY

Maybe we could pretend for a few
minutes before you go to sleep:

You could be King or a General,
and I could be all your Merry Men.

Or we could wonder together what
would happen if white boots didn't
make footprints in the snow, and no
one knew where we were going to go.

Or you could explain to me where
the dust in old houses comes from
when there's no one living there.

And before Mom comes
in here
in a couple of minutes
to kiss you good-night
and empty all the neat
                                        pieces
and starting
                    parts
of your soul
from your dunagree pockets,
I could teach you how
to set mousetraps. . . .

LETTER TO PETE

Sorry for not writing.
I have not been myself lately.
The weather is as fine as I hope
you are. I still love you.

I've been working hard.
I've been working hard and
I've been happy, but
I have not been myself.

What are you doing,
in your own way?
How's your love?

One can refuse or give
everything to a brother
because he will still be
your brother . . . .

Brother,
friends understand because
they try. Brothers understand
anyway?

My brother, what
can I say? Remember,
I need you there.
I will try.

Love, your
brother.

EIGHT STANZAS CONCERNING THE GREAT "WHO ARE YOU?" AND "NAME THE LITTLE ANIMALS" CONSPIRACY

Ask "Who are you?"
at any toddling toddler.
And if you bring it up right,
the kid'll grin at you.
But he won't know, either.

Nobody else asked me. I was different.
'Cause there were two of us.
Brother Bob and me.
My twin. We grinned, too.
And asked each other.

It's like that, being a twin.
You sort of know.
And soon as you can talk,
you each introduce each other
to whoever you meet.

I'm Bob's brother
and he's mine, except being
a twin, it's like growing up
with your best friend
sleeping in the bunk above you.

And you're never ever afraid
of the dark, and the two
of you can beat up
any kid on the block,
but you never ever need to.

And you have twice
as many friends
as most folks, and folks
get sick of you twice
as fast. But you never ever do.

And right from the start
you stand apart together
on a pair of separate leashes,
or lie in a double pram
kicking each other with answers.

So even now
he's married and gone,
I still reply to both names,
and say I'm housebroken,
and still sort of know.

EASY TO SHARE NOTHING

An old girlfriend I went through
school with, still take
out now and again, teaches
Grade One at our old grade school,
naively believes in trust.

"The most important thing
in the world to remember is Trust,"
she says, holding an American penny
in her hand in class. "See?
IN GOD WE *TRUST!!*" And the kids giggle.

After school she asks what I
was doing last night, really.
And because I trust her
I tell her the truth
as if she didn't exist . . . .

ALONE POEM

Even with all the lights on,
I'm alone.
Alone with myself.
Not the kind of alone
when all you've got to do is get up
and go, go out in the hall and holler
for the love who's always there, so
it's really safe, after all, to lie
on your back in the dark and wiggle
your toes under the blankets.
No,
this kind is the kind that starts you
wondering if maybe this is the way
you've always been, a no-kidding
kind of alone.
There's no
such thing as "present," after all,
where you're the only one here.
You're so
alone you don't know who you are.
There's no
one to holler to, now.
Are you reading
this poem because you're alone?
I'm writing
it because I am.
Can anybody write
a poem in the dark?

NEXT TIME I WON'T WRITE IT

I sit up alone smoking
late at night, trying

to figure out how I've
failed at being a human

being with other people,
decide that anybody can be

human in a poem, that
it's much harder to be

someone who's human in-
side himself, and that

poems are only as inhuman
as their readers. I read

this one as I write it
to decide if it'll be

detached enough from me
to show anyone. Maybe, I think,

(At the moment it doesn't
look as if it'll make it.)

what I need is a good friend
who doesn't understand

a thing he reads, or do I
need a woman who

can save my poetry
by killing me?

PROMETHEUS, 1957

Brian Atkinson was Wayne's older
brother, and it was when we were eleven,
and Brian aspired to climb where he wasn't allowed to go
up the DANGER – HIGH VOLTAGE tower
by the woods by the tracks late
one Saturday morning some seventy feet up
and we all heard
                                        when he slipped and grabbed power in
an arc of jabbering humming light looking up there
and shrank so small that when we went to see where
his body had fallen, the indent hole in the ground
was about the same size as a baby's body,
and we all heard how he was burned to a crisp
at school that Monday, and everybody knew
Wayne that much better.

THE DOG

Someone said, "You know, Bill,
dogs are dogmatic: you can tell
a lot about the master from the dog."
So I bought the dog, brought him up
to act in such a way that everyone
would love him, taught him
magnificent tricks, and fed him
only the best dog foods. Everyone
in town knew my dog and loved him,
threw sticks across fields for him,
and shook their heads and smiled
when he never brought them back
to them, always brought them home
to me. And when I left that town,
I gave my dog to my best friend,
and now, I understand, he brings sticks back
for everyone.

GREY WOMAN

Tight, time is up lips
on that grey woman with half a beard,
the one with Mrs. in front of her.
Can't imagine who'd marry or name a woman
like that, or how, now a widow woman
with no smiles. We clash, alone together,
each meeting a parting, wide
and wild eyeing each other to see
who tells the first lie.
She clips and slices words at me
like unsafe razors to be returned
dulled or sharpened by my will.

Words to others flow from her
like seconds from electric clocks
about my flaws. She hates me
because I'm rash enough to write, breaking out
enough to be right. I tell myself
an old woman is never someone
to get along not getting along with, still
I wonder why I don't ever smile
back at her when she doesn't. I hate her,
try to write her out of me,
words choked in endless draftings,
suddenly many times her same age,
practising my rightness.

I study the fading grey, the vital question
she asks with her eyes without her mouth
knowing or caring to ask it, study without
knowing what a real student is,
and break it down . . . .

Smiles are always young,
hold tears like cups until someone
turns them upside
down over impossible lifetimes.

Once she was young, she says:
soon I'll be old, I'm told.
And if no matron is a mother,
then no poet is a son.

SECOND APPROACHES

When I was almost twelve,
the blackest hand there is scooped
me up and started squeezing hard, and since
hands aren't ears, it doesn't help to scream,
and the older I get, the harder
it is.

When Old Fred Henderson passed
away, it took his wife just six weeks
to do it too, but when I went past their Grand
Old House, the veranda rocking chairs were still
moving with the need of the passing
wind, and of giving it
a sound.

When she backrubs me,
she always takes her time
away by taking off my wristwatch,
before she begins, and afterwards
I sometimes dream
of roses.

AN INTERVIEW WITH THE FIRST STAR OF THE EVENING

The game is over, and all
we have now is tonight's score,
forgotten by the end of the week.

But he's the guy who waltzed right
in there, between the raw eggs
and hot pennies, when the teams
were back on the ice, to our right
and left, in the trinity of time
zones, changing on the go, and
failing to capitalize:

"If we can get the team together,
you know, we can make the playoffs,
eh?"

But then was seven in the morning
at the Shirley Street Arena, so cold
your breath stared back at you
in amazement and your feet
never woke up . . . .

And once I shook hands with him.

AT THE CARNIVAL

It's all before you all
at the carnival:
                                There are men there
who know how
                                  to throw real knives
and make them look real.
And women so good
                                           that they are
                                           what they are.

THE BORDER

Our Side:
Here we all are, dodging
myths instead of bullets.

Their Side:
When the best minds leave
they leave the rest behind
forever?

THIRTY UNDER THE WEATHER POEMS

(Lines Composed Upon The T.T.C. At Various Suppertimes Over A Two-Year Period)

Section One: *Trolley Poems*

1.
Bread in the oven.
Mostly dirt roads and dogs.
A neighbour on the phone.
The lap you don't have
until you sit down. . . .

2.
The yellow-white grass
      that isn't hay
because it isn't cut.

3.
The Pollution Index is 38.
This is peaceful non-existence.

4.
The reality   she gives   to things
just by   touching   them.

5.
Police apprehensions:
A life insurance salesman
away on business forever.

6.
Children are daypeople.

7.
It's a job to get a job to get a job to retire.

8.
Radio is the television of the mind.

9.
The sweet peace
after the burial
of the baby.

The long war
we were all
born after.

10.
HE
HE
HE
HE
HO HO HO HO HOME ME ME ME ME
OM
OM
OM
OM

11.
The red fox in his forest:
Trees older than the men
who dare to cut them down.

12.
She's playing the same
solitaire game as you.

13.
Payday is walking home
on the rooftoops of cabs.

14.
A small animal overflowing
your arms
            with an extremely long tail.

Section Three: *Streetcar Poems*

15.
She's as preoccupied as any man
toting a ten foot two-by-four
in his teeth.

16.
Woman-figure hills: Waiting
for the sky to make up
its great grey mind. . . .

17.
A wine so fine
            it goes
to your heart
            instead
of your head.

18.
Inadvertent Advertisement:
A drunken sailor
on the make on
the train

19.
I will hold it
as long as I can I will
hold it as long
as I can

20.
You can't do dope for a living.

21.
The floorplan
for your castle
on the ceiling
of the sky.

22.
Your father's outstanding success
in badminton?

23.
It's almost as if love
kept good time.

Section Four: *Subway Poems*

24.
The industry of dusk, the dust
on your windowsill, a small bird
you can't name: A speck of dust
in the eye of God.

25.
If God is dead, where
can I send the flowers?

26.
The force of love
instead
of the love
of force.
Love
clubbed by words
left
unsaid.

27.
The old folks would call her
a character builder.

28.
Their process has now taken over:
Like barbarians, we're cheating each
other in order to survive. . . .

29.
Even the blind speak of insight.

30.
Finding yourself is mostly a matter
of remembering where you are, and who.

WHY MY MOTHER'S SECRETLY AFRAID

You can't breathe and drink at the same time.

Meanwhile I'm going blind.
The Monkey Demons are learning how to swim.

I still need a shower and two big meals a day.

I still have a few things left.
The connections between my muscles and bones are aching.

I don't know the things I do.

I keep forgetting.

LOVE SONG OF THE SPINSTER SPIDER

Sleep, a craven image
of itself, creeps
from your bloodstream, not
the pain, just the memory
of the memory of the dream
of the pain you remember.

You remember the possibility
of the dream, the myth
you've left behind, the spider.

You dreamed you were awake,
remember?

And over your head, above
your sleep, the spider
put my End to her web, while you
fixed her in your dream.

She was just as big
as your face below her, and she
slowly spiralled toward the hugeness
of the hole in the centre
of your face
and faced you.

You stared up, back
against the hugeness
of the hole above you,
and her eyes met yours,
black with hate.

                    You fell
awake when she fell
on your face in the dark, below
the myth, before it.

Remember?

And then the morning:
you wake up and discover
you've had explorers
in your bloodstream.

First you find the patch
of dried blood on your right
wrist, then the patches
on your pillow, and maybe
the ones that haphazard the upper edge
of your top sheet.

You carefully search your body
to find out where
you bled from
sometime in the night.

Morning becomes the discovery
that something has escaped
from you, it's waking up
and making up your reason why:

Whatever exists, only exists
when it continues, only continues
when you wake and find you've been
dying again, is only dead
when you can't find traces, is only traced
when you return, is only traced
when you return

AFTER THE ONE ON THE LEFT HAS LIT YET ANOTHER CIGARETTE

You remember a few small things, now
that we've left you.

                                        For example
the floor of the room. Or perhaps
the scratches
on the bottom of your metal plate. . . .

But none of these things are unlikely.

What mattered most at the time
was what you'd think of it all/if
you could recall anything
                                                    else.
We knew *everything* about you,
then. . . .

ACID SPACE

We speed beyond ourselves,
beyond the atmosfear, faster
than the speed of ultra-
violent lite. . . .

Tomorrow never needs
to know how often. . . .

So much of what we need
has no need of us.

WELCOME TO THE CORPORATION.

1. Here is a list of your securities.

2. We fired a man to make room for you.

3. We think that much of him. Personally, he

4. may come back to haunt us, but we hope he's tired.

5. You're overqualified, but young people come cheap.

6. Don't spend too much time with wrong numbers.

7. We like to keep our value systems systematic.

8. There is no better way for getting things done.

9. We protect our own best interests. Most people

10. settle down into less than who they are.

11. They're vulnerable, our best customers.

12. We solve the mechanics of living for them.

13. Our competition has gone too far. . . .

ON THE NATURE OF HUMAN FAME

To look again at nature, to see
in hindsight the un-
forgotten nature of living
things. . . .
                    Oh God, what have I
done to the language
of my country-
side?
    The root verbs of my garden
fight each other for life
in the dark of my mind as I turn
over in my sleep. . . .
                                        Thank God
for the roots of trees and men
who need them.

ANOTHER MEAL

"I only kill what I can eat."

America, I watch you from your north,
terrified that I will go down with you,
and there is a great violence inside me.

"We'll pay for everything we destroy."

I no longer trust myself beside you,
with your armies of innocent individuals,
and your means to kill my way.

An old friend is the best of all enemies.
Some of my best friends have left you.

We eat what we are. . . .

PIAPOT, SASKATCHEWAN, CANADA

for Dale Zieroth

Alone is a prairie experience.
Soon there'll be more people than trees.

NINE EXTRA NOTES

for Anton Kuerti, Pianist
and Tony Kuerti, Man

Like you, I too
am hungry before

you begin, for yours
is the dis-

tinction between
art and artifice

peace and pace, time
and tone, dis-

cipline and decency, food,
and nourishment. (When

you play you ride
borrowed horses

pound legs off
personal instruments

wear your peace
button like a halo

and introduce me
as your friend.)

You show familiarity
with Empire, for yours

is a smokeless fire.
You have nine extra

notes you never need
to stop. For the song

is not implied
until the last chord

echoes the last word.

POEM FOR GLEN THE LIAR

Now, all of us know Glen
is a notorious bull-shitter,
but before he killed himself
this time, he got through
and took me with him.

He was saying great music wasn't
lost in the air and gone, that he
could store it up inside himself
and dig, say, Stravinsky, who he likes,
any time he wants.

So even when we asked him
to prove it and he couldn't,
I believed him this time:
there was music in the way
he told it.

WHETHER REPORT

(The Fall of Québec Revisited)

It won't be long
now before
the leaves
turn brown
from green

like the highway
signs along
the 401
from Toronto to
Montréal,

between
two cities, a season,
a winter no

one wants

a border. . . .

Why
must my country always be
my corner of my country?

HOME MADE KISSES

You met the night before she said
she loved you, and all the scars
of context in her eyes turned blue
from grey when you kissed her. She
arched her end of everything toward you
with the promise that she needed nothing
more than this, and soon your needs
were nothing. Right away you made love
in a world full of people making love
without too much to make love from,
and then you came to sleep tonight
in each other's secret arms.

And then the morning found you
with forever's good intentions, still
woke and left you with the question
of whether you should hold her for
now, or until there's nothing left
of your distances, and you lie alone,
outside the closeness of your fear,
inside the silence of your eyes.

But she's grinning again and her eyes
are still blue, and you
can't compete with yourself inside
yourself this morning, so you grin back
and grab her again, and you feel
like a bunch of whistling kids.

OUR TIME OF NIGHT

Dear Beverley,

It's Canadian as hoping for what
you can expect. I haven't shaved
for two days. Love, my distance
away from you is measured by the hair
I have to add to your old picture
in the wallet of my mind. (Don't cut your hair
until I'm back.) I have two beers
in my belly and you on my mind.
                                                  But being here
is important, too.
                              Here, the mountains
describe themselves for the first time.
And even the foothills are as high
as anything I've ever seen before.
                                                  Being here
is so important, I almost forgot to tell myself
where I'm from. But where you're from
is nowhere near important as where
you're going.
                        I'm three time zones
from home and still trying. . . .

And there's little time left for poetry when
you're driving a grand piano across
the Rockies in early March, hon.
                                                  I'm concentrating
on the piano, which I can't play, rather
than the truck, which I can't play, either.
                                                          It takes
a lot of time and mind to stretch yourself further
than a thousand miles and still be
in the same place.
                              I go 70, try
to beat the night into the mountains . . . .

Tonight is falling. (Our Time Of Night, remember?)
And time is the shock of distance, hits
with fists fast as lightning
in a day sky.
                    But the truck is its own
time warp, now.
                          So now we can make or take all
the time in the world, to get our zones of thought
together.
             And here we are, vague as the distance
between us, sure as eating, sleeping, waking
up, and moving on . . . .

If only I could take all these spruce trees,
the tallest I've ever seen, along the way
now, and turn them into ideas
for us.
          I'm afraid of the dark.
                                        And it's getting
darker. (Are you still with me, really?)
I feel doomed enough to try to make friends
with what I can still see
of the mountains beside me.
                                        But the mountains
are friendly only up to their treelines . . . .

Grinning at a mountain is like deciding to dedicate
a poem to someone only if she first agrees
to misunderstand it . . . .

Our headlights, switched on
for safety's sake an hour ago, are just
starting to show.
                          They give just enough light to see
the whole country in the map of the mind, with all
its time zones drawn in.
                                   And the further we go, the more
we have to use our high beams.
                                          We pass three
sports cars, each with skis, and a chartered

bus, barely believing its way along.
                                        We like to think
the people who pass us know their way better
than we do, for it's still impossible
to cross this country
without an Indian guide . . . .

And the road does decide where the mind
can go.
      Like "what one woman has reported
to be a rabid fox" on the radio outside Sudbury.
Or maybe the World's Largest
                                    Stuffed Moose
in Dryden. And most certainly, the Queen
Elizabeth II Coronation Commemorative Post Cards
with eighteen years of prairie road dust on them
"flown by aeroplane to Dundee"
                                      and
                                          "on sale
in London by 11 o'clock"
                              a few short hours
after the event, back at some small
town, back there . . . .

What Rockies???
                      At night
they move in on you like myths.
                                      I swallow
my way up.
            I cleared Calgary at five, a football
field frozen hard
                      as the last instant
                      of the last instant
replay.
      The prairies were a great frozen lake.
                                        Someone
said I should make Revelstoke by eleven.
                                            Maybe

I'll learn something before I'm over
and on my way down.
                                I'm alone now, driving
the great curve of Canada, with
myself.
        You . . . .

You're right when you say
there's a lot that doesn't need to try
to be explained because
we both grew up from the same
place.
      But my freedom demands experience.
                                                We've met,
and yet there's so much more
to be explored, so much more
that has to ease its way
along . . . .

            ICE.
                        In order to get and keep
control of this truck I have to start with
myself.
        I clutch myself in
and out of gear.
                        I am what I drive as well as how
and where and why.
                            When will I make third?
                                                    Everytime
I change my beams they look whiter.
                                            Inside
the dream, the engine of the dream
is labouring.
                    I'll be scared of myself by the end
of tonight . . . .

Even if I've never seen it,
I can smell the Pacific.

Ever since Winnipeg.
How can you have a Pacific dream
with only an Atlantic memory?
And yet we learn
to love from memory.
We do it alone, I guess, until
we come to what we both have known . . . .

AVALANCHE AREA!!!
And though it's a Federal Park
they don't allow you to stop.
A straight stretch.
Four snowsheds, sign "Lights?"
Another straight
stretch, and I'm already doing 60 when I think about
unlocking the other side
door, *hell*, *all* the doors!!
So that when
I get caught
in an ava-
lanche they'll
(whoever *they* are)
be
(whenever they *find*
me)
able
(*if* they find *me*!) to get what's left of me out
easier.
If a man is too late for his own ideas
of terror, then maybe he's ahead
of other people's . . . .

But here I still am.
It's amazing anyone would
pay me to do this.
Three antelope know enough to keep out
of my way.

Highway signs, visible again, skeletons
just before they're gone, flash past.
And all miles
are measured equally on the speedometer's odometer.
This might be more democratic if the speedometer worked
properly.
More animals, eyes of animals, ideas
of themselves . . . .

Now, except for the odd trailer trucker,
I have the whole treacherous road
to myself.
They're considerate with their headlights,
sometimes seem surprised to meet me, coming
this way this early.
When I reach the highest point
on the Pass, the piano behind me will sound
a C Major
(muffled by the wind and its covering).
And
the truck
(which I'm not concentrating on)
will gently
slip off an icy patch
frozen there specifically
for me.
And I'll continue on in the air with the chord
for some unspecified lifetime . . . . . .

I wonder what he was thinking, the guy
in the fur parka back there. Did he
notice me? I stop for a leak
now, in spite of the signs.
There's Orion, the Hunter.
I've never felt or been
as close to him before.

Or you. People who
drive trucks have
character.
Love,
Bill.

THE WOMAN

No, you are not like
other women . . . .

Your
weather falls on me. I
feel it outside there.

I dream about your smell.
Even with the lights on.
Even in the afternoon.

My body has another
secret name for you.

SKIN DEEP

My mind's eyes are open.
My time wanders
along the fine line of you . . . .

The problem was your beauty.
I was terrified. And yet
it was all part of you.

We had to invent a new way.

Now we have your answer
to my question. Now we
make love with our bones.

POEM ABOUT HER UGLY GIRLFRIEND

Which I suppose will show how
intolerant I am. But it does
bring up the question
                whether or not
I like someone simply
                because I'm supposed to?
And why some people are born
beautiful while others simply acquire
                                ugliness?
(But: "She's a nice person, though . . . .")

When I was younger I was expert at undoing
bra hooks
        with my eyes. All of which has nothing
to do with me
            waiting for her
                        to get off the phone.
(I can tell by her tone who's on the other end.)
I only know whatever
                I do from here on afterwards
will be wrong. (Hello,

Hello?) Now I age everytime the phone rings.
(It seems I have a great *ugliness* inside me.)
But I'm a nice person, though . . . .

LIES

God knows you know me . . . .
More
telling lies are more
often told
in the dark of day
than the light of night.
Yet sickness
always seems to come
by night . . . .
Beginnings and endings,
stoppings and startings.

I know what it's like
not to have you
to explain.
I don't know what I mean.
I get that scared.

I go through it alone,
while you want us
to do it together . . . .
Can I do it
with you?

HI

It's a matter of fabrics
of feeling, of trying
to figure into what's implied
from what is left unsaid . . . .

Sometimes
I feel so useless, unable
to help you with your womanhood
as you share with me my manhood.

And yes, look,
I've just cleaned off all my wouldbe
whiskers from the sides of our
bathroom sink this morning,
with Ajax.

So please don't ask me to blame you
for being you. Then, I'd have to love you
like a little boy.

And are we playing house?

THE CONTINUING SAGA OF SIR LITTLELANCE AS TOLD IN SERIAL FORM TO THE MAID BEVERLEY

Sir Lancelot (Do you Lancealot?) returns
home from his grailing trail and finds
his castle and his lady in ruins,
the result of a plundering blunder by
his arch-rival, the evil Black Prince.

What about her chastity belt? Well,
the Black Prints caught her in the chamber
with the special magical key he'd stolen
from Merlin the week before.

The castle can wait. Launcelit leaves
immediately to revenge himself (in hot
pursuit) of Melvin. Meanwhile
you have a huge hole in your pantyhose. . . .

CLUMSY WOMAN

Here is another shiny
personal object for you
to break:

(That first night
the light caught you
in a certain
appealing angle.

Now, no matter what
you do, assuming all
your angles, postures,
unexplained reactions,
the light stays with you.)

I am blind with it, with
you, see only who
you are and what
you do.

THE PARTICULARS

We started with God.

Now we have gotten
down to particulars.

We remember about dentists.

We leave each other
money and cigarettes
for the morning.

MRS. HOWELL'S MYSTERY POEM

1.
To start, she says she
doesn't know anything
and then she tells me
why:

It takes a whole minute
on the phone at noon
to get out
of our lunches
and into
our own voices/

and on the subway after
unhappy-ending movies
we ride home under
the weather
together . . . .

2.
She's in the shower
listening
to the sound of the water
under her showercap . . . .

But she also washes, rinses, hangs, and leaves
her hair in the kitchen sink.

And she puts bookmarks in conversations
and forgets to lock her bicycle
and the phone's in her name.

But she's almost perfected her own
glaze and her wicks are getting
straighter all the time.

And she's always shy when
she's only wearing
her bare feet . . . .

3.
Sweeping floors is shit work.
Especially when you're alone.
At least we're not waxing now.

Or I forgot the groceries again.
Her list burns its own hole in my pocket.
Now I have to invent the truth . . . .

4.
And saying it is useless
unless it's either unexpected
or unnecessary.

CONTINUING POEM

We have come a long way together.

We have come back home so often
we know the way by heart.

Now she wears a nightgown.
I have given her my cold.

We continue . . . .

INSIDE OUT ON YOUR OWN

The wall of your love beside you
has memorized your shadow, you
have stood alone that long.

Alone in starless chaos, you
have shared enough dreams, have
become yourselves instead of each
other's ideas of each other.

You have taken your time and said
with your needs for tomorrow what
words will always try to say.

You have listened to her summer
wind in the leaves of your evening
mind, and seen the morning mist
that clears itself before her
mystery.

And now your world empties out
of itself inside itself, inside
a snowstorm of stars.

Your shadow shields her world
with sleep, and asleep she loves
to believe in you.

Sweet peace ascends all
along the line . . . .